THE SECRET LIFE OF PAUL REVERE

HERO OF THE AMERICAN REVOLUTION
BIOGRAPHY 6TH GRADE | CHILDREN'S BIOGRAPHIES

DISSECTED LIVES
auto biographies

First Edition, 2020

Published in the United States by Speedy Publishing LLC, 40 E Main Street, Newark, Delaware 19711 USA.

Dissected Lives Books are available at special discounts when purchased in bulk for industrial and sales-promotional use. For details contact our Special Sales Team at Speedy Publishing LLC, 40 E Main Street, Newark, Delaware 19711 USA. Telephone (888) 248-4521 Fax: (210) 519-4043. www.speedybookstore.com

10 9 8 7 6 * 5 4 3 2 1

Print Edition: 9781541950931
Digital Edition: 9781541952737

See the world in pictures. Build your knowledge in style.
www.speedypublishing.com

TABLE OF CONTENTS

In this book, we're going to talk about the life of Paul Revere, so let's get right to it!

WHY IS PAUL REVERE FAMOUS?

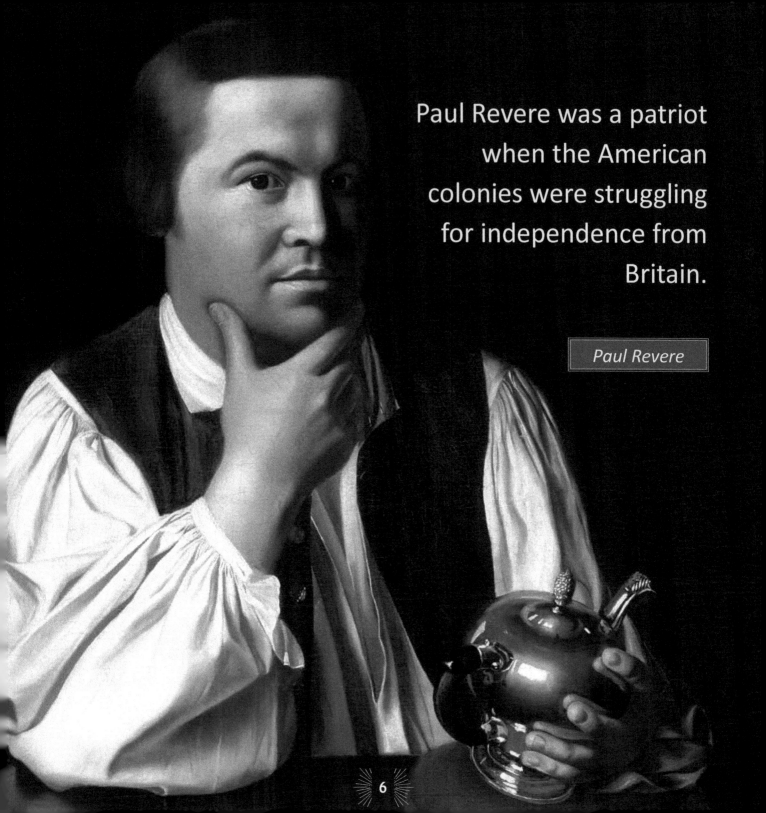

Paul Revere was a patriot when the American colonies were struggling for independence from Britain.

Paul Revere

He was known locally in the Boston area, but it was a poem written by Henry Wadsworth Longfellow that made Revere nationally famous.

Henry Wadsworth Longfellow

The poem was penned in 1860 and then published in the *Atlantic Monthly* magazine.

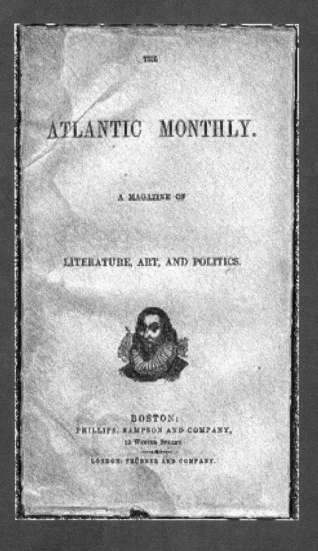

Longfellow, like many great writers, didn't get all the details correct. But the poem, called *Paul Revere's Ride,* made the midnight ride that Revere made on April 18-19, 1775 to the city of Lexington famous. When it was published, it was more than 80 years after the night of Revere's ride.

like a pall on sculpture, till another man took the burden from him and went up to the house with his dead.

When Mr. Raleigh entered the house again, it was at break of dawn. Some one opened the library-door and beckoned him in. Marguerite sprang into his arms.

"What if she had died?" said Mrs. Purcell, with her swift satiric breath, and folding a web of muslin over her arm. "See! I had got out the shroud. As it is, we drink *skål* and say grace at breakfast. The funeral baked-meats shall coldly furnish forth the marriage-feast. You men are all alike. *Le Roi est mort! Vive la Reine!*"

PAUL REVERE'S RIDE.

LISTEN, my children, and you shall hear
Of the midnight ride of Paul Revere,
On the eighteenth of April, in Seventy-Five:
Hardly a man is now alive
Who remembers that famous day and year.

He said to his friend, — "If the British march
By land or sea from the town to-night,
Hang a lantern aloft in the belfry-arch
Of the North-Church-tower, as a signal-light, —
One if by land, and two if by sea;
And I on the opposite shore will be,
Ready to ride and spread the alarm
Through every Middlesex village and farm,
For the country-folk to be up and to arm."

Then he said good-night, and with muffled oar
Silently rowed to the Charlestown shore,
Just as the moon rose over the bay,
Where swinging wide at her moorings lay
The Somerset, British man-of-war:
A phantom ship, with each mast and spar
Across the moon, like a prison-bar,
And a huge, black hulk, that was magnified
By its own reflection in the tide.

Meanwhile, his friend, through alley and street
Wanders and watches with eager ears,
Till in the silence around him he hears
The muster of men at the barrack-door,
The sound of arms, and the tramp of feet,
And the measured tread of the grenadiers
Marching down to their boats on the shore.

Then he climbed to the tower of the church,
Up the wooden stairs, with stealthy tread,

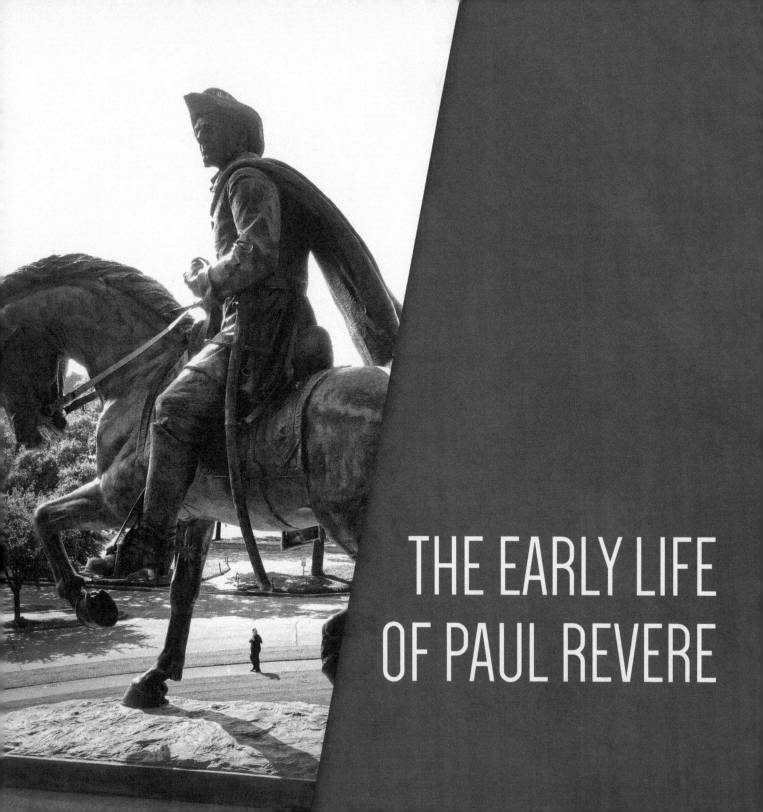

THE EARLY LIFE
OF PAUL REVERE

Even though the exact date of Paul Revere's birth isn't known, he was born in late December of the year 1734.

Paul Revere

His father, Apollos Rivoire, was a French immigrant who was a goldsmith. He "americanized" his last name to "Revere" after he had lived in the colonies for some time.

Paul Revere's father was a goldsmith

Paul's mother was the daughter of a colonial family of artisans. Her name was Deborah Hichborn.

Deborah Hichborn

Eventually the couple had many children. Paul Revere was the eldest of their sons who had survived and the third child who had been born to them. In those times, many children died at a young age and never reached adulthood.

Young Paul Revere

Although Paul Revere's birthplace isn't known, what is known is that his father moved both their home and his workshop from Boston's center, at a location called Dock Square, to the North End of the city in 1730.

Aerial view of North End and Italian District, Boston, Massachusetts

Hanover Street, Boston
Massachusetts

16

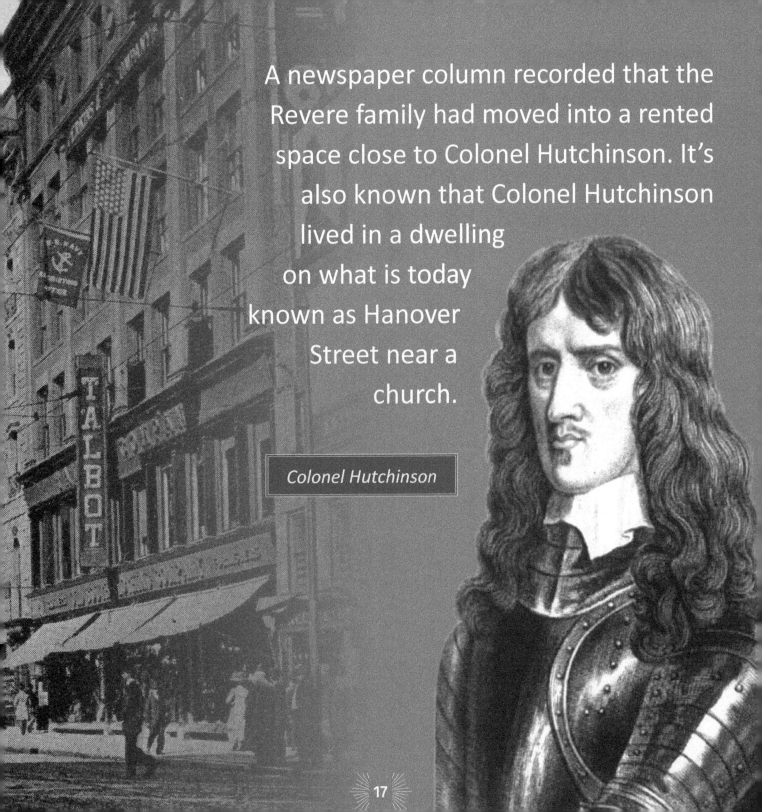

A newspaper column recorded that the Revere family had moved into a rented space close to Colonel Hutchinson. It's also known that Colonel Hutchinson lived in a dwelling on what is today known as Hanover Street near a church.

Colonel Hutchinson

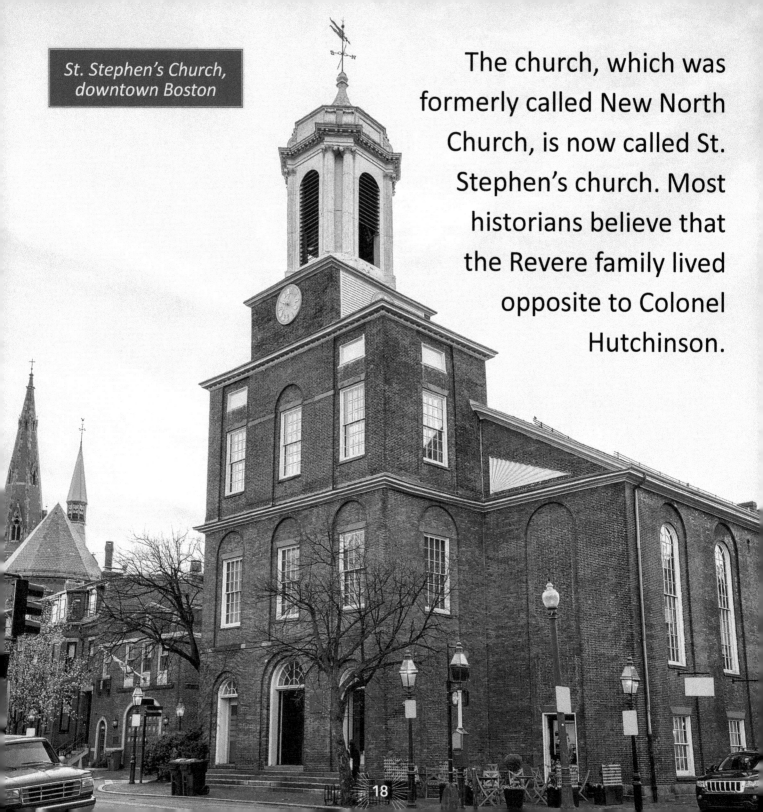

St. Stephen's Church, downtown Boston

The church, which was formerly called New North Church, is now called St. Stephen's church. Most historians believe that the Revere family lived opposite to Colonel Hutchinson.

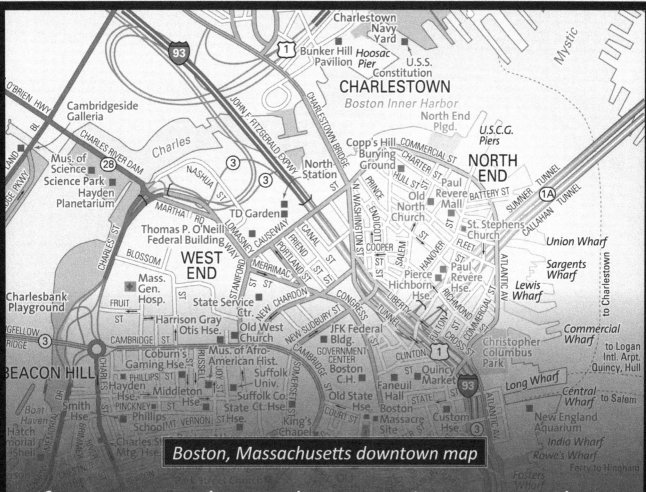

Boston, Massachusetts downtown map

If you want to locate the approximate area where they lived on a map of Boston today, you could find the location near the intersection of Tileston Street and Hanover Street.

1972 Paul Revere Silversmith .999 Fine Silver
38Grams Silver Medal

Paul went to school at the North Writing School, but he learned his trade from his father. He worked with gold and silver. Today, this profession is known as a silversmith. He continued his training until he was 19 years of age. At that time, tragedy struck and his father died.

Paul had to jump into his role to make money to support his siblings. At the age of 21, he was commissioned to join the artillery in the state of Massachusetts as a second lieutenant. In upstate New York, he fought French soldiers, even though his father had been French.

Revere joined the artillery as a second lieutenat

He came back to Boston in the autumn of 1756. At that time, he worked hard to build up his family's business and he became known as a master silversmith.

Paul Revere silver collection, Worcester Art Museum, Massachusetts, USA

At the age of 23, he married Sarah Orne. He had eight children with Sarah and six of them survived. After Sarah passed away in 1773, he married Rachel Walker. She took care of him as well as the six children he had had with Sarah. Paul and Rachel also had eight children together and five of them survived into adulthood. In order to support his large family, Paul had to work very hard.

Rachel Walker

On North Square, a block from the waterfront in Boston, the original home where Paul and his extensive family lived is still standing. When he bought it, it had already been around for 90 years!

Paul Revere House, Boston Massachusetts

Its upper story is a larger size than its lower story. The windows are a diamond shape. It's the oldest house in Boston.

Family Living Room

Fireplace in the Living Room

Paul Revere's chamber

There were plans to tear it down in the year 1902, but Paul's great-grandson bought it. Then, he worked to create an organization to preserve the house as a monument and tourist attraction.

The oldest house in the city of Boston, built in 1660

If you go to Boston, you can visit it. Paul's family was not the first family to live there and after they were long gone, many others lived there. Today, the house is staged so you can see some of the furniture and other items that belonged to the Revere's.

Paul Revere's house is one of the tourist attractions in Boston

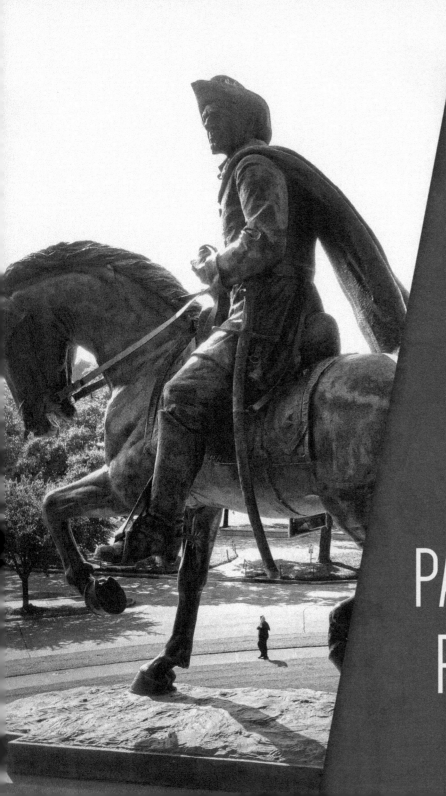

PAUL REVERE'S PROFESSIONS

Being a silversmith was Paul's primary vocation. He worked with gold, silver, and copper, but didn't work with pewter. His shop was the center of his work life for over 40 years. Paul was a master of his craft.

An image of a silversmith working

He employed others to help him, but he was responsible for the quality of every piece from the simplest, everyday spoon to tea sets worthy of the wealthiest families. He was also responsible for the quality of the metal alloy that was used to produce his pieces.

Revere's silver shop

During his lifetime, his work was highly regarded. Today some of this masterworks sell for over a quarter of a million dollars.

> *Some of Paul Revere's pieces have very high monetary value*

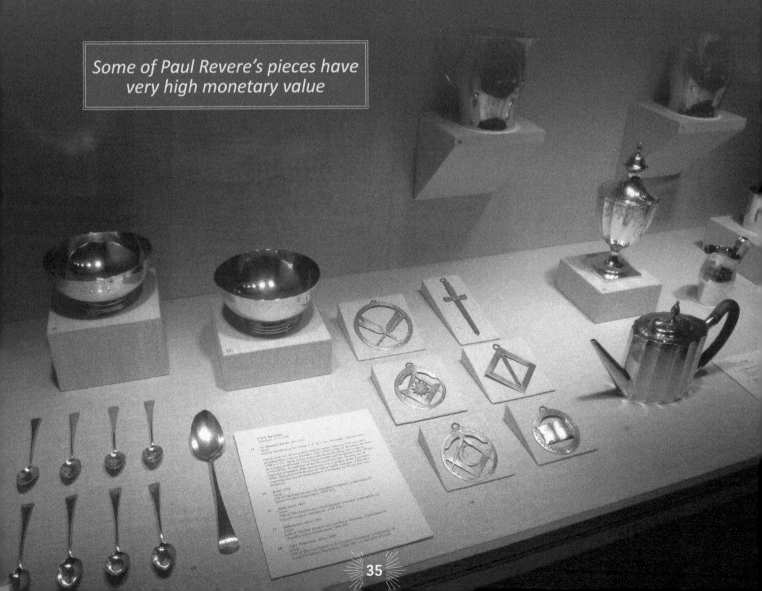

After the French and Indian War was over in 1763, there was an economic depression. Paul needed more income for his family so he began to branch out. He started to work at engraving copper.

The original plate of Paul Revere's Boston Massacre engraving

He created engravings for book and magazine illustrations. He also created business cards for his clients and political cartoons.

Paul Revere Engraving from original 1767 Plate The Harvard Book 1st Edition

Political cartoon "The wicked Statesman, or the Traitor to his Country, at the Hour of Death"

He produced bookplates, a book of songs, and bills used for taverns.

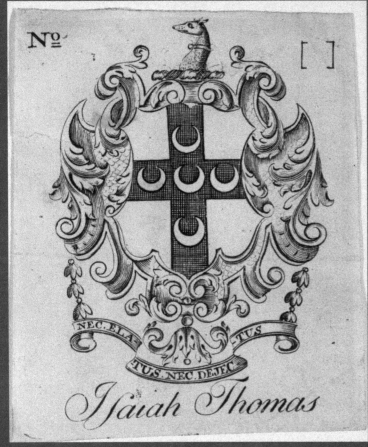

Bookplate for Isaiah Thomas

Bookplate for David Greene

Bookplate for Epes Sargent

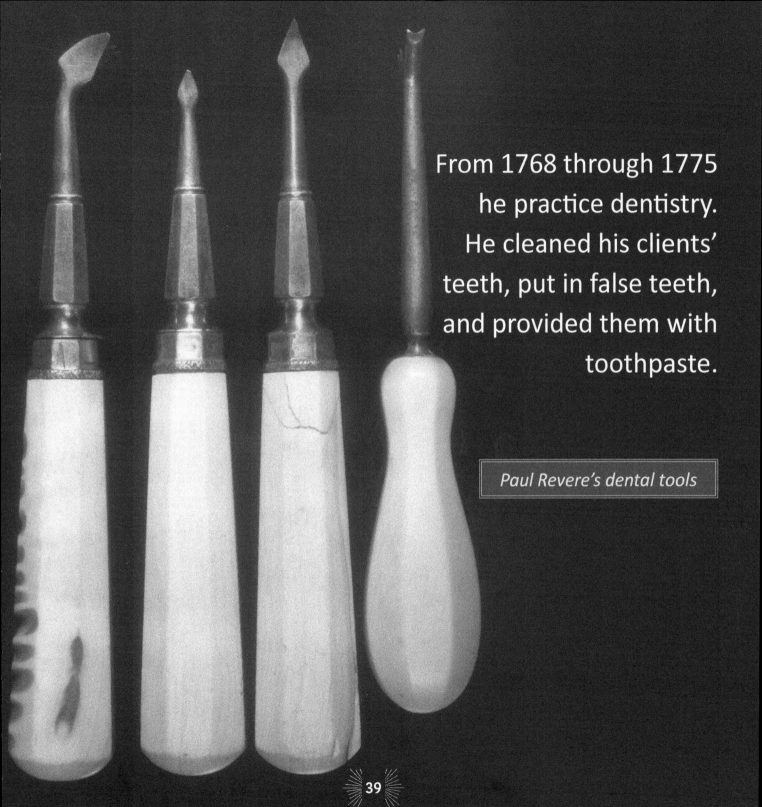

From 1768 through 1775 he practice dentistry. He cleaned his clients' teeth, put in false teeth, and provided them with toothpaste.

Paul Revere's dental tools

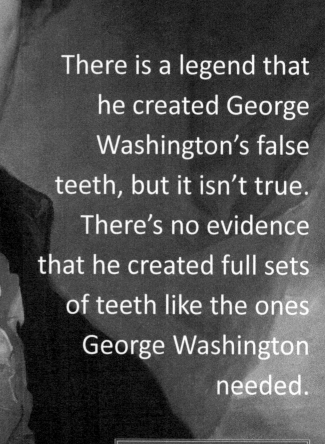

There is a legend that he created George Washington's false teeth, but it isn't true. There's no evidence that he created full sets of teeth like the ones George Washington needed.

George Washington

Some of Paul's sons came to help him in his business as well. In the Beacon Hill neighborhood of Boston, there is a historic building called the Massachusetts State House.

Massachusetts State House

The cornerstone of the building was secured there by Samuel Adams in 1795.

Samuel Adams

In 1802, Paul Revere and his sons coppered the building's dome.

Massachusetts State House Dome

The Museum of Fine Arts in Boston has a priceless Sons of Liberty bowl that Paul Revere engraved with the names of 92 men who were patriots and helped to build the United States.

Paul Revere's Sons of Liberty Bowl

PAUL REVERE'S POLITICAL AFFILIATIONS

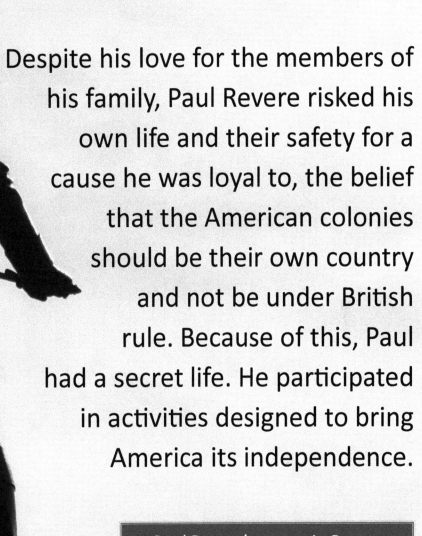

Despite his love for the members of his family, Paul Revere risked his own life and their safety for a cause he was loyal to, the belief that the American colonies should be their own country and not be under British rule. Because of this, Paul had a secret life. He participated in activities designed to bring America its independence.

Paul Revere's statue in Boston

Paul became politically active through his connections with local groups and his business clients. He was a member of St. Andrew's Masonic Lodge and there he met an activist by the name of Dr. Joseph Warren.

St. Andrew's Masonic Lodge in Massachusetts

In the year prior to the Revolution, Paul collected intelligence useful to the patriots' cause by documenting the movements of the British militia. He was a courier for several important state-organized committees and made a regular run with messages to the Continental Congress, which was located in Philadelphia.

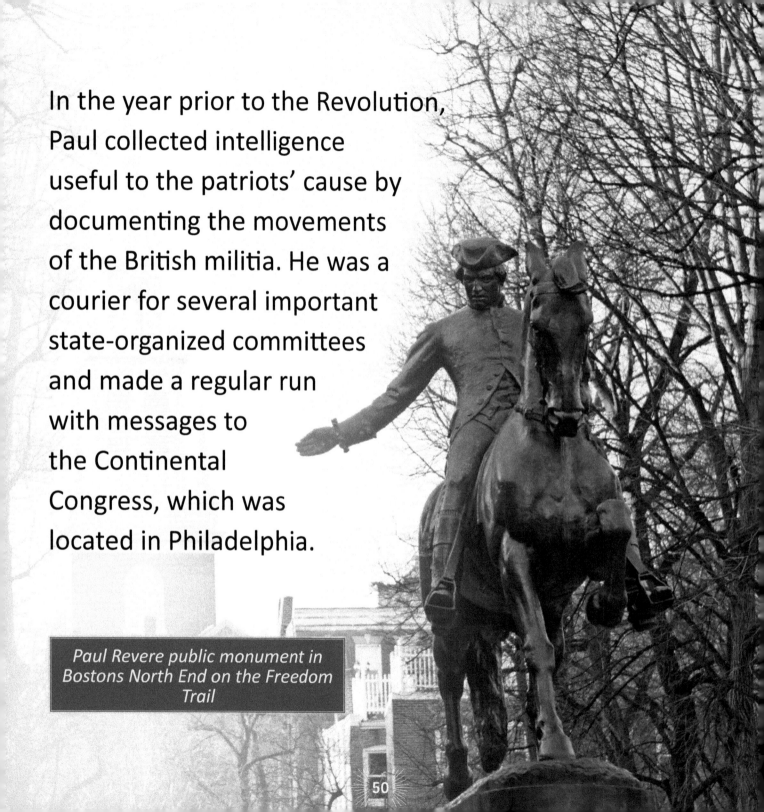

Paul Revere public monument in Bostons North End on the Freedom Trail

With other Boston activists, he helped plan the demise of the East India Company, which produced tea.

Coat of arms of the East India Company

The Tea Act ensured that the colonists must keep this British company from bankruptcy by buying their tea at the exclusion of all others. The colonists rebelled by throwing 92,000 pounds of tea overboard into the Boston Harbor.

Wooden chest East India tea crate

Paul spread the word regarding the event, later called the Boston Tea Party, by riding to New York and also Philadelphia.

The Destruction of Tea at Boston Harbor

THE MIDNIGHT
RIDE

Paul Revere was made famous because of his midnight ride, which took place on April 18-19 of 1775.

Paul Revere's midnight ride

At that time, the British soldiers were occupying Boston under the command of General Thomas Gage.

General Thomas Gage

The colonists felt that the conflict was inevitable. They had tried diplomatic means to gain what they wanted, but it hadn't worked. They had begun to stockpile weapons in preparation for an upcoming war. Many of the weapons had been stored in the city of Concord, about 20 miles away from Boston.

Aerial view of state and city buildings, Concord, New Hampshire

General Gage had plans to seize the ammunition, but the Sons of Liberty found out about those plans through their network of spies.

The Sons of Liberty pulling down the statue of King George III on the Bowling Green, New York

Paul Revere gathered together a group of riders. Their job was to warn patriots John Hancock and Samuel Adams. They had set up a plan with lanterns to be lit in the Old North Church in Boston.

Paul Revere waiting for the signal from the Old North Church Tower

Revere commanded the Charlestown militia to look for a sign in the window every night. One lit lantern would mean the British were coming by land and two would mean that their plan was to cross the Charles River. On the night of April 18, British soldiers placed their boats from the docks into the water, so it was clear that their plan was to travel by sea.

Revere commanded the Charlestown militia to look for a sign in the window every night

Robert Newman, the church's caretaker, and Captain John Pulling Jr., who was Paul's close friend, scaled the ladders in total darkness. The climb was almost eight stories. They lit the two lanterns for just one short minute, but it was enough for those watching across the river in Charlestown to see.

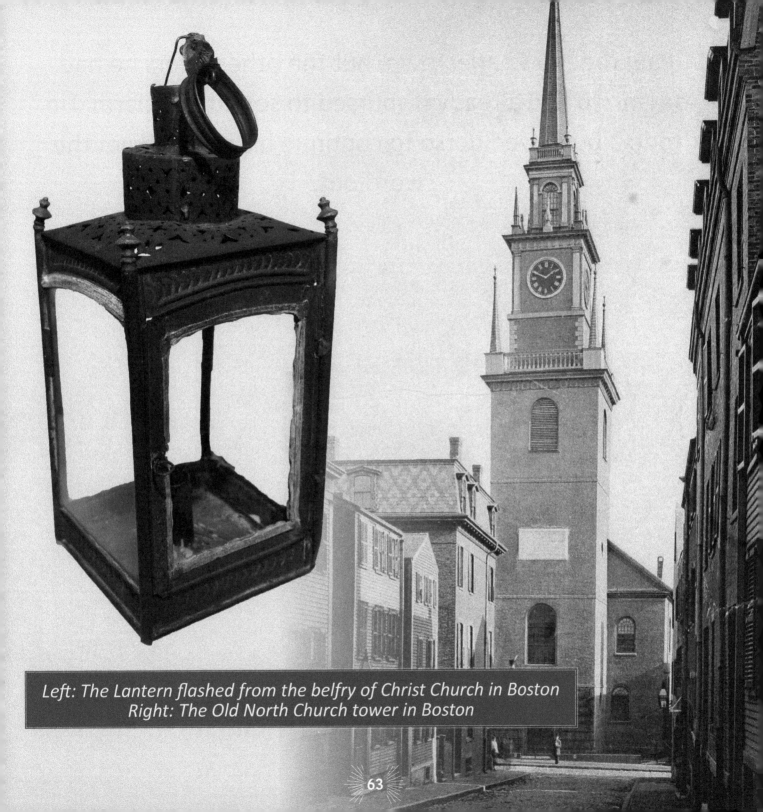

Left: The Lantern flashed from the belfry of Christ Church in Boston
Right: The Old North Church tower in Boston

Paul rode to Charlestown, but the other riders he had organized had already disbursed to sound the alarm. He rode a borrowed horse to continue his ride and get the word out.

That night, the group of riders carried the message
from New Hampshire all the way to Connecticut

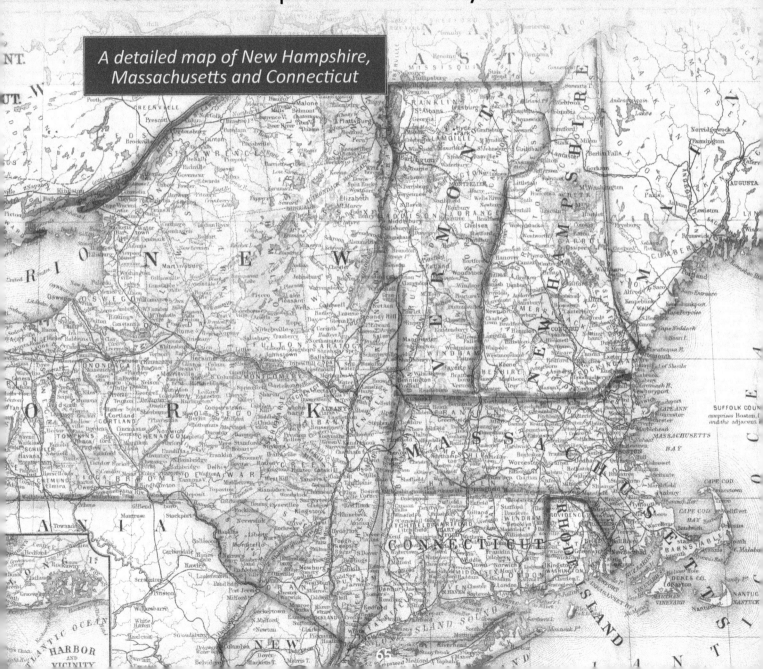

A detailed map of New Hampshire,
Massachusetts and Connecticut

The Battle at Lexington

When the British showed up to seize the ammunition, the armed colonists were waiting for them. This event was the start of the Revolutionary War and it was the night that made Paul Revere famous.

PAUL'S LATER LIFE

Paul continued to serve the cause of independence as part of the militia. In the years after the Revolution, he expanded his business. He opened a hardware shop in Boston's downtown area.

Paul Revere

By 1788, he had started a foundry, which made nails and spikes for Boston's ships

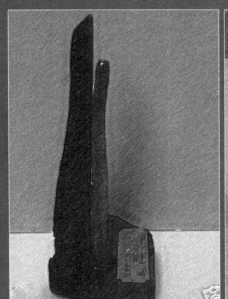

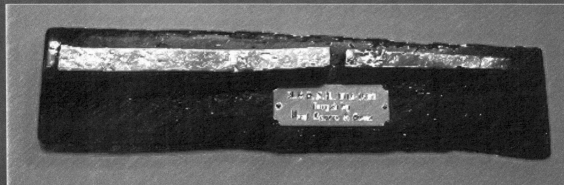

Copper Spikes And Bronze Nails By Paul Revere

He produced cannons and bells as well.

Paul Revere's Artillery Cannons

Paul Revere House "Revere Bell"

He also opened the first successful copper mill in the colonies in 1801 and provided copper sheeting for the famous ship the *USS Constitution*.

Edward H. R. Revere, the great-grandson of Paul Revere at the plaque dedication of the rolling mill on April 20, 1951

Paul Revere tombstone at Granary Burying Ground in Boston

He passed away in 1818, at the age of 83 and is buried in Boston's Granary Burying Ground.

SUMMARY

Paul Revere came from a large family and had a large family of his own. He was a silversmith by trade, but he also had a secret life. He participated in activities to help the American colonies become an independent nation. He gathered intelligence, acted as a messenger and organized other messengers, and fought as part of the militia. He risked his life for America's independence.

Awesome! Now that you've learned details about the life of Paul Revere, you may want to read about the American Revolution in the Baby Professor book, *US and British Military Leaders during the American Revolution - History of the United States | Children's History Books.*

Visit

BABY PROFESSOR
EDUCATION KIDS

www.BabyProfessorBooks.com
to download Free Baby Professor eBooks and view
our catalog of new and exciting Children's Books

CPSIA information can be obtained
at www.ICGtesting.com
Printed in the USA
LVHW021936130122
708483LV00005B/160